STOPS:
40 Encounters to the Cross

STOPS:
40 Encounters to the Cross

Marty Dunbar

Marvin United Methodist Church
2014

Copyright © 2014 by Marty M. Dunbar

All rights reserved. This book or any portion thereof may not be reproduced or used in any manner whatsoever without the express written permission of the publisher except for the use of brief quotations in a book review or scholarly journal.

First Printing: 2014

ISBN 978-0-615-96245-0

Marvin United Methodist Church
300 W. Erwin St.
Tyler, Texas. 75702 www.marvinumc.com

Dedication

To Jami, my soulmate and wife. Without you, I would never be the man I am. God is so good, and you are one of the great blessings I have received from Him.

Thank you, Dr. Doug Baker, Marvin UMC, and all those who inspire me every day. Most of all, I am thankful to my Heavenly Father, who gave me and all the world the greatest gift in Jesus.

Contents

Marty Dunbar

Author's Note

THIS BOOK IS A LENTEN DEVOTIONAL MEANT TO BRING YOU CLOSER TO THE STORY OF JESUS THROUGH CONTEMPLATION, STUDY OF SCRIPTURE, AND PRACTICAL APPLICATION OF FAITH.

The title of the book comes from a passage of scripture found in Matthew 20:29-34. Jesus and his disciples were leaving Jericho and heading to Jerusalem. He had made many STOPS along His ministry. This encounter with two blind men would be one more of those life-giving STOPS on His way to the cross.

The two blind men were destitute and desperate for something to change their lives. They heard that Jesus was coming *(remember, they could not see Jesus coming)*. They yelled at the top of their lungs, like we might shout for our favorite football team when they score a touchdown. Their shouts were embarrassing and telling. This is what desperate people do. They were not reverent or formal, they were in need—and now everyone would know it.

15

They did not want anything spiritual, they wanted to be healed of their blindness. They wanted to be able to see. Verse 34 in chapter 20 says, *"Jesus had compassion on them and touched their eyes. Immediately they received their sight and followed him."* (NIV)

This story sets the tone for our journey through the season of Lent in the Christian Church. We start on Ash Wednesday, proclaiming our need for repentance and a call to believe the Gospel. Every day is a journey towards the cross, the tomb, and the resurrection of our Lord and Savior Jesus Christ. As we journey, we see our great need for Jesus. Just like the two men in the scripture passage, we are in desperate need of a touch from Jesus.

This book contains 40 STOPS Jesus made along the way to the cross. I believe people are desperate to know that Jesus still STOPS for them.

Each one of us at some point on our journey of life and faith are the crowd, the beggar, or even the one who STOPS.

Instructions

Every devotional day focuses on one of Jesus' STOPS on His way to the cross. Each day includes an encounter found in one or more scriptures, a short reflection, and a suggested song to go along with the encounter.

This devotional starts on Ash Wednesday and concludes on the Saturday before Easter Sunday. There is not a devotional for any of the Sundays during the season of Lent. Each Sunday is a day of celebration of our Lord's resurrection and should be spent in worship with other believers at a church.

At different times, there will be special instructions to engage in a spiritual discipline beyond contemplation, prayer, or scripture study. There will be times of fasting and a call to service. Most days include multiple versions of the same scripture story. You may choose to read one, or choose to read them all.

There is also a suggested musical selection. You may find these on any online music service, on iTunes, or on YouTube.

Day 1 // Stopped to Party

Scripture Passage: John 2:1-12

Jesus begins his public ministry with a STOP at a wedding. He STOPS to party with his disciples and family members. The wedding couple has run out of wine, which is a social embarrassment, and Jesus' mother (possibly a family member of the bride and groom) knows someone who can do something about it.

After a short exchange with Jesus, Mary steps out in faith and boldly instructs the servants "do whatever he tells you." (2:5) Mary does not challenge Jesus' authority; she simply steps out in exemplary faith. Mary has no idea of how Jesus will solve this embarrassing social problem for the wedding couple, but she trusts that He has the resources to do it.

She then calls the servants to an open-ending obedience to Jesus. To *do whatever He says* is the trademark of every committed disciple of Jesus. At a party in Cana, Jesus STOPS to share fellowship and ultimately calls those He encounters to faithful obedience. Jesus is calling each one of us to faithful obedience. It is open-ended and leads to places many of us could never have imagined. It leads us to people and encounters we never would have planned. May your day be filled with encounters in which you are eager to trust and be obedient to Jesus.

Musical Selection: *Holy is the Lord*
                            by Andrew Peterson

Day 2 // Stopped to Worship

Scripture Passage: John 2:13-22

Jesus STOPS to worship at the temple in Jerusalem. When God shows up to a worship service, He wants to see people praising, repenting, praying, and offering themselves in Spirit and in Truth. This day, Jesus had enough of the traditions of the people at the temple. The sacrificial system of the Jews had become a pyramid-scheme for the temple priests and the moneychangers. People would come to the temple from throughout the known world to offer sacrifices to God for their sins.

Worshipping God is about expressing our love and adoration for him. As Christians we are called to follow Jesus, and we become the offering and sacrifice. The Apostle Paul says this in Romans 12: "Be a living sacrifice." Jesus has never accepted the lives of people that try to buy or earn their way into His presence. Jesus simply wants a heart that is yielded to obedience and grace: a heart and life that proclaim, "I worship because of what God has done for me on a cross."

Musical Selection: *The Heart of Worship*
by Matt Redman

Day 3 // Stopped to Share New Life

Scripture Passage: John 3:1-21

Jesus STOPS to share how every person ever created can have new life. Jesus is a savior and friend. God's will is that no one should perish. (Peter 3:9) You would expect a Savior to offer a way to salvation, and Jesus shares the secret to this life of salvation with Nicodemus. Jesus not only shares the secret to salvation but also reveals the very purpose for which He has been born into our world. John 3 verses 16 through 17 are called "the gospel in a nutshell." God loved the world, gave His Son, and whoever believes will not perish but have eternal life. God didn't send His Son to condemn a sinful people, but to save them through believing in Him.

Every day, we encounter a situation or a person who needs the hope of Jesus. What situation in your life needs new life given by Jesus? What relationship needs the hope of Jesus? What person needs you to love them and not condemn them? Who has God brought to you today?

Musical Selection: *Blessed Assurance*

Day 4 // Stopped to be Rejected

Scripture Passage: Luke 4:16-20

Jesus STOPS to proclaim He is God! And He does it in his hometown, to the people that He grew up around and played street ball with on the corner. This sort of proclamation would get most of us thrown into the nuthouse. For Jesus, it almost got Him killed. He also experienced heart-felt rejection from those who knew Him deeply.

Jesus' ministry and life was filled with rejection. Over and over in the gospels, He tells the disciples that people will reject Him. Finally, His rejection leads to death on a cross.

Have you ever been rejected by another person? It hurts, and it can leave scars on our lives. Most of us are dealing with different scars from rejection. Maybe it is from a group of people who did not accept us as a child or teenager. Maybe it is from a parent or boss who we could never fully please: someone we respected or respect, and we care deeply about what they think about us. Most of us do not want to admit it, but we do seek approval from others. And when they reject us, it hurts, and it scars.

Hebrews 4:15-16 speaks of Jesus, who is our High Priest, who understands our weaknesses and can empathize with our human experiences. Jesus wants to touch you and heal you of your scars and brokenness. He has experienced rejection and failure, as each one of us has in the past or present. Do not let rejection by another stop you from embracing the life abundant given to us by Jesus. Jesus is ever-present and is willing to set the captives free. Turn to Jesus and find wholeness, healing, and full acceptance from the Creator of the Universe. That truth will set you free!

Musical Selection: *Through the Night*
by The Digital Age

Sabbath Day // Stop. Rest. Worship.

Come, let us worship and bow down.
Let us kneel before the LORD our
maker.

– Psalm 95:6

Day 5 // Stopped to Heal

Scripture Passage: Matthew 8:14-17, Mark 1:29-34, Luke 4:38-41

Jesus had a mission to take away the sins of the world and to bring spiritual, emotional, and physical healing to those He encountered. In America, we tend to think healing miracles are merely a New Testament practice that does not occur in our modern world. This is far from the truth. Every day across America and this world, God is physically healing people. The evidence of healing is multiplied as you go into third-world countries that lack the medical resources of Americans. Missionaries continue to share stories of people being healed from cancer and fatal diseases.

In America, we see medicine, technology, and the medical professionals who use these products to heal people every day. Why do people not attribute God's healing power to the advancements in medicine and technology? Is it because many of the people who develop and use these never profess a faith in God? Whatever the reason, maybe it is time for followers of Jesus to step up and give credit where credit is due, to the Creator of the Universe. God is the great healer and the great physician. God gives people the ability to research and develop. That does not come from some random Big Bang.

As society becomes more advanced in healing the human body, let us never forget that God wants all people to be whole. Let us take the time to praise God for the medical professionals (doctors, nurses, techs, and hospitals) who bring healing to the human body and mind. Let us also remember that God wants us to bring our prayers of healing to Him.

Who can you pray for that needs healing?

Maybe you need healing, and so can pray for yourself?

The reality of this world is that the believer will not always find the healing they want on earth, but ultimately will only find this healing in Heaven. Praise God for Jesus Christ, who gives us forever-healing.

Musical Selection: *Healer*
by Kari Jobe

Day 6 // Stopped to Forgive

Scripture Passage: Matthew 9:1-8, Mark 2:1-12, Luke 5:17-26

Christians are taught to be good and nice. Actually, all people are taught to be good and nice. When we hurt someone physically or emotionally, we are told to say, "I am sorry!" But merely saying you are sorry does not make it better for the one who was hurt. When you ask someone to "forgive you," it puts the power in the other person's hands.

"Forgiveness doesn't excuse their behavior. Forgiveness prevents their behavior from destroying your heart." Many of us have the need to forgive another person. They hold power over us because we are not willing to forgive. Our lack of forgiveness destroys our hearts.

God is the great forgiver. Jesus displayed this truth on the cross. God has forgiven us and calls us to forgive others. We receive undeserved forgiveness; may we share it with others.

Musical Selection: *Forgiven*
by Bethel Worship

Day 7 // Stopped to Call

Scripture Passage: Matthew 9:9-13, Mark 2:13-17, Luke 5:27-32

Jesus STOPS to call a sinner into His ministry. Before Jesus, no one would have ever imagined a savior like Him. No one even imagined a God who cared so much about His own creation. This was a game-changer. Do you know what a game-changer is? It is the play or decision in an athletic event that turns everything around for those who are losing. Until Jesus came, sinners were losing.

In the scripture passages for today, Jesus calls one of His disciples. Matthew is a chief of sinners because he is a tax collector. He cheats his friends and fellow Jews out of money in the name of Caesar. In this encounter, Jesus calls Matthew to "follow him." No one before Jesus would ever have thought about asking a tax collector to be a disciple. But Jesus has come for the loser, the broken, the destitute, and the sinner.

If you consider yourself a follower of Jesus, you have been called to a glorious mission. You are a part of the Body of Christ. Plan A to change the world. You are a part of the hope of the world, the Church, the Body of Christ. Do not be timid in this call! Jesus needs you to be bold and go into the world proclaiming the good news. This world needs good news and that good news is the ultimate game-changer, Jesus.

Musical Selection: *I Will Rise*
by Chris Tomlin

Day 8 // Stopped to Fast

Scripture Passage: Matthew 9:14-17, Mark 2:18-22, Luke 5:33-39

Jesus' ministry began with a fast. He was in the desert for forty days and forty nights fasting in preparation for His public ministry. Fasting is spiritual discipline still used by believers today. Many believers choose one thing to fast from during the season of Lent.

The founder of the Methodist Movement was John Wesley. Wesley created a style of fasting that encourages the participants to pray more deeply. What is the Wesleyan fast? The Wesleyan Fast begins on Thursday evening, after dinner. It continues until mid-afternoon on Friday. During this time you do not take solid food, but instead use the time allotted for eating to focus on prayer.

As a follower of Jesus, you are invited to fast from one thing during the season of Lent or participate in Wesley's style of fasting.

Musical Selection: *Holy Spirit Have Your Way*
by Leeland

Day 9 // Stopped to Proclaim

Scripture Passage: John 5:16-47

Jesus STOPPED to teach people who he was as person and what His role was as the Christ. The theological term Christology is defined as the branch of Christian theology relating to the person, nature, and role of Christ. What you believe about the person, nature, and role of Jesus is vitally important to your faith and how you see God. Jesus' life was a picture of who God is and what God wants for His children. Jesus was God in flesh. Jesus showed us that God seeks a relationship with each created being. He created them, loves them, and wants to spend time with them.

As Christians, we believe that Jesus Christ is our Lord, who was conceived by the Holy Spirit and was born fully human and fully divine. He came to die for the sins of the world on a cross. He is the ultimate atonement for our separation from God. By his work, we are saved and redeemed. The person of Jesus Christ was both fully human and fully divine in one body. Jesus was fully human, but was also God incarnate—God "in the flesh." The gospel of John refers to this doctrine: *"And the Word be-*

came flesh and lived among us, and we have seen his glory, the glory as of a father's only son, full of grace and truth." (John 1:14 NRSV)

Jesus felt that what we thought about Him and what people thought about God was vitally important. May we all be a reflection of Jesus, today and every day.

Musical Selection: *At Your Name*
by Phil Wickham

Day 10 // Stopped to Eat and Drink

Scripture Passage: Matthew 12:1-8, Mark 2:23-28, Luke 6:1-5

Jesus STOPS to do a very ordinary thing, and the Pharisees (religious police) become very upset. Why? The Sabbath was the day of rest. No faithful Jew was supposed to work, but Jesus ignores this tradition and picks grain with His disciples as they walk through the fields. Sounds pretty rebellious, don't it? It was to the lawmakers, but not to God.

Jesus said He came to fulfill the law, not to abolish it. (Matthew 5:17) He actually meticulously kept its requirements (such as circumcision, presentation at the Temple, and visiting Jerusalem on feast days). He also came to free people from religious bondage and unreasonable demands from religious leaders. Jesus kept the moral law but challenged the hypocrisy of the religious leaders.

Never allow yourself to fall under religious bondage. May you claim freedom in grace through faith in Christ alone. (Eph. 2:8-9)

Musical Selection: *by the Grace of God*
by Gateway Worship

Hallelujah!
Praise God in his holy house of worship, praise him under the open skies; Praise him for his acts of power, praise him for his magnificent greatness; Praise with a blast on the trumpet, praise by strumming soft strings; Praise him with castanets and dance, praise him with banjo and flute; Praise him with cymbals and a big bass drum, praise him with fiddles and mandolin. Let every living, breathing creature praise God! Hallelujah!

- Psalm 150

Day 11 // Stopped to be with Others

Scripture Passage: Matthew 12:15-21, Mark 3:7-12, Luke 6:17-19

Jesus STOPS to find a little alone time, and a crowd follows Him. He feels compassion for them and begins to heal those who are sick. We all need alone time, but not at the sacrifice of our relationships with others.

The Christian faith is a faith lived out in the company of others. Actually, the Christian ethic found in the Sermon on the Mount (Matthew 5-7) is an ethic lived out in the context of a community of faith (a church).

Jesus always put people before Himself. This is not an easy thing to do in our fast-paced society. May we be challenged to STOP and spend time with those whom God has put in our path today.

Musical Selection: *If We are the Body*
by Casting Crowns

Day 12 // Stopped to Visit with the Enemy

Scripture Passage: Matthew 8:5-13, Luke 7:1-10

Jesus STOPS and talks with an enemy of His people. The Roman centurion was a leader of troops. He was a man who represented the physical oppression of the Jewish people. The Roman government ruled with an iron fist and never apologized about it to anyone. In actuality, this commanding soldier was Jesus' enemy in society. Nonetheless, Jesus STOPS, listens, and heals the centurion's servant.

Who will you encounter today that you or another have labeled an "enemy?" Is there someone who has been your enemy for so long that you do not even remember why that is? Live your life free from fear of people. Live your life in freedom to reach out to all people in the name of Jesus.

Musical Selection: *A Mighty Fortress is Our God by Martin Luther*

Day 13 // Stopped to Consult

Scripture Passage: Matthew 11:1-19,
Luke 7:18-35

Jesus STOPS to consult with the disciples of John the Baptist on whether He is the messiah or not, which sounds a little strange. Was not John the one who proclaimed the coming of the Messiah and, by baptizing Jesus, publically proclaimed that Jesus was the Messiah? Yes!

John (Jesus' cousin) has been arrested and is sitting alone in a dark, cold, scary, disease-infested jail cell. John is merely human like you and I, so maybe this experience has shaken him to his very core. Maybe he is beginning to doubt what he has already professed and claimed in his life.

Does this ever happen to you? Do you feel doubt when suffering and trouble comes into your life? Doubt is a normal aspect of faith. Take time to consult a friend in the faith. Spend time in fellowship with other believers and watch how God can use this time to reassure you of His mighty promises and presence.

Musical Selection: *All the Power and Powerless by The Digital Age*

Day 14 // Stopped to Share the Truth in Love

Scripture Passage: Matthew 11:20-24

Jesus STOPS to warn specific communities that they are not on God's side and will not fare well during the final judgment. Jesus did not go around judging people, He was seeking to liberate sinners from their sins. On this occasion, Jesus is speaking the truth in love. He was not going to let these communities live in sin any longer, He was going to warn them and call them to repentance.

Jesus wants us to live a Godly life, A life in step with God's moral will for His children. He has made provisions for our holiness and purity by dying on a cross as a sacrifice for our sins. Jesus does not just want to forgive us, He wants to purify our hearts. He wants to sanctify us, by taking the sin out of us.

May the Holy Spirit speak into your life with conviction and love, showing you the sins you need to repent of and ask forgiveness from. God has made these evident in love, not in condemnation.

Musical Selection: *For the Sake of the World*
by Bethel Live

Day 15 // Stopped to be Thankful

Scripture Passage: Matthew 11:25-30

Jesus STOPS to be thankful for His heavenly Father. Pastor Andy Stanley said, *"Unexpressed gratitude, communicates ingratitude."* Does our worship communicate gratitude towards God? Does our life communicate gratitude towards God? What about our prayer life? Our gifts to the church? Are we expressing our gratitude, or are we filled with unexpressed gratitude?

Just because we feel grateful, doesn't mean we actually are grateful. May this day be the day we express our gratitude to God and to others. Jesus does not want us to live life filled with unexpressed gratitude.

Musical Selection: *Once Again*
by Matt Redman

Day 16 // Stopped to Love a Sinner

Scripture Passage: Luke 7:36-50

Jesus STOPS to love a woman no one else wants to love. Jesus encounters a woman so distraught by her lifestyle and past sins that she is moved to anoint His feet with oil and clean them off with her hair. Jesus is in the middle of an important dinner with important people. This action was simply humiliating for the woman. The host of the dinner party was not humiliated; rather, he was disgusted with Jesus because Jesus allowed himself to be touched by this sinful woman.

How does Jesus handle the situation? He handles it like He is a friend of sinners. He forgives the woman of her sins.

You and I are sinners. The Apostle Paul says, "We have all fallen short of the glory of God." (Romans 3:23) He tells us that sin continues to reign in our flesh-nature, and that it is fighting the Spirit-nature present in our salvation. But He gives us power to overcome temptation, and Jesus has defeated the death brought about by sin. Sin remains! But Jesus Reigns! Claim this victory!

Musical Selection: *Carried to the Table*
by Leeland

"The highest form of worship is the worship of unselfish Christian service."

- Billy Graham

Day 17 // Stopped to Teach

Scripture Passage: Matthew 13, Mark 4

Jesus loved to teach using parables. Parables are stories that illustrate a point. As a follower of Jesus Christ, we are called to be His disciples. Disciple means student. As followers of Jesus, we are called to be life-long learners or students of Jesus. The Bible is the inspired Word of God, written over a 1000-year period. When Christians study the scriptures, the Holy Spirit will speak into our hearts and minds for the present realities. This makes the Bible the living Word of God.

Christians need to be learners of God's word. We need to read it, study it, and discuss it in groups with other believers. The teachings of Jesus are not to be left on a shelf or hidden away in our brains. They need to be lived out every day in faithful obedience and eagerness.

Musical Selection: *How Firm a Foundation*

Day 18 // Stopped to Calm Storms

Scripture Passage: Matthew 8:23-27,
Mark 4:35-41, Luke 8:22-25

Right about now, you have either come through a storm in your life, are going through a storm, or have a storm brewing in your future. This is the reality of life. The storms of life come in many different forms. The severity of a storm depends on the individual person. Some storms seem intense during one season of life and less intense during another.

Even as followers of Jesus, we will face the storms of life. In our scripture lesson for today, Peter and the disciples are reminded that Jesus can calm the storms. Jesus does not cause every storm, but He is strong enough to deliver us from the storms. The Apostle Paul affirms this in Philippians 4:3: "I can do everything through him who gives me strength."

When the storms of life are beating us down and we doubt our survival, we can turn to Jesus. We can call out to Jesus for help. He will be there to strengthen us!

Musical Selection: *It is Well*
by Todd Fields

Day 19 // Stopped to Mourn

Scripture Passage: Matthew 14:3-12,
Mark 6:14-29, John 11:1-44

John 11:35, "Jesus wept," is the short-
est verse in the Bible. Jesus was fully human
and fully divine. Jesus knew what it meant to
lose people whom He loved. Before Jesus was
thirty years old, He had already lost His father,
Joseph. by the time He was thirty-three, His
cousin John had been executed, and His good
friend Lazarus had died. Luckily for Lazarus,
Jesus called him back out of the tomb.

Jesus STOPS to mourn those He loves.
He knows the deep feelings that come from losing a loved one. He has encountered the gut-
wrenching feeling of grief and life-change that
comes from death.

In *20,000 Days And Counting*, Robert
D. Smith, says, *"I know I will die, but I do not
know how long I will live."* We are all going to
die. So may we live life to its fullest in Jesus.
When death invades our space, let us claim victory over death through faith in Jesus.

Musical Selection: *Great is thy Faithfulness*

Day 20 // Stopped to Feed the 5000

Scripture Passage: Matthew 14:13-21,
Mark 6:14-29, Luke 9:10-17, John 6:1-15

Jesus STOPS to feed over 5000 people moments after He finds out that His cousin John has been executed. Despite his efforts to be alone, Jesus is followed to a place that lacks the resources to feed the crowd following Him. In the midst of his grief and his time of mourning, Jesus still cares for God's children.

Is there a person or a situation that needs your attention? Have you been ignoring it? Pray about what you need to do and then do it. God will honor your prayers and your effort.

Musical Selection: *Amazing Grace*

Day 21 // Stopped to Walk on Water

Scripture Passage: Matthew 14:22-33,
Mark 6:45-52, John 6:16-21

Jesus has fed the 5000 and wants to find some time alone. He has been waiting for this moment of solitude since learning of John's death. He makes His disciples get into the boat without Him, and sends them away. He dismisses the crowds and goes up the mountain to pray by himself. We see Jesus modeling what He taught His disciples earlier in Matthew 6:6: *"But when you pray, go away by yourself, shut the door behind you, and pray to your Father in private. Then your Father, who sees everything, will reward you."*

Jesus then jumps onto His very own personalized jet skis (his feet) and heads out over the water. This encounter was a miracle, and the disciples react appropriately to it, with awe, wonder, and worship.

May your day include solitude with the Heavenly Father and when you worship, let it be filled with awe and wonder because of the miracle Jesus has performed in your heart.

Musical Selection: *Oceans
by Hillsong United*

Day 22 // Stopped to Touch Others

Scripture Passage: Matthew 15:29-31,
Mark 7:31-37

Jesus STOPS to feed more people, but He spends His time healing them through touch. Jesus was a man of compassion and He loved to share His compassion through the ministry of touch.

Research shows that people who struggle with anxiety in their lives need the ministry of touch. People who are dealing with a loss or an overwhelming situation react very positively to a hug or a hand on the shoulder. Research also shows that their heart rates come down when another is willing to touch them appropriately out of love and concern.

Many of the people you will encounter today need a Christ-like touch in their lives. People who might come to mind are those who live alone, who are battling an illness, who have had recent tragedy, or who are living through a storm in their lives.

Musical Selection: *Here in Your Presence
by New Life Worship*

Sabbath Day // Stop. Rest. Worship.

"Our entire being is fashioned as an instrument of praise…when we use body language to express praise, that which is internal becomes visible."
- Lamar Boschman

Day 23 // Stopped to go to the Top

Scripture Passage: Matthew 17:1-13,
Mark 9:2-13, Luke 9:28-36

Jesus is getting closer to Jerusalem and Good Friday. Most of us can only imagine what might be going on inside His mind and heart. God the Father knows what is going on inside and gives Jesus a reminder and a glimpse of Heaven. God the Father gives Jesus a mountaintop experience. Jesus visits with Elijah and Moses. Jesus is transfigured as a foretaste of His resurrected body. The experience is so over-the-top that Peter wants to set up a camp and stay in the moment.

God is a gracious God. He gives us glimpses of Heaven along our journey of life. He allows us to enjoy mountaintop experiences through a mission trip, baptism, worship service, youth camp, or retreat.

Nonetheless, though we would love to stay on the mountaintop, real life is lived in the valleys.

Musical Selection: *Never Once*
by Matt Redman

Day 24 // Stopped to Visit Friends

Scripture Passage: Luke 10:38-42

In Joanna Weaver's book, *Having a Mary Heart in a Martha World*, she says, *"The world clamors, 'Do more! Be all that you can be!' But our Father whispers, 'Be still and know that I am God.'"* Mary and Martha find themselves in the presence of Jesus. Mary is welcomed by Jesus to sit at His feet like a disciple, and learn from Him. Martha is also serving Jesus in her own way through the gift of hospitality. Martha believes that Mary should be serving in the same style, so she asks Jesus to set Mary straight.

Jesus' reply to Martha seeks to express that all followers of Jesus have been gifted for service. Serving God through our gifts is always honorable. If our service to God has become busywork void of devotion to God, we are serving out of the wrong motives.

In what ways do you serve the Church? Are they for your benefit or for God's? Do you seek glory for yourself or for God?

Musical Selection: *Carry Your Name*
by Christy Nockels

Day 25 // Stopped to Teach Prayer

Scripture Passage: Luke 11:1-13

Prayer is the spiritual discipline given to us all to communicate with God. This spiritual discipline is essential to a dynamic and vibrant relationship with God. There are many formulas or exercises in prayer that you can use. Saint Ignatius' exercise in prayer is called the Examen Prayer:

Thanksgiving - *Lord, I realize that all, even myself, is a gift from you.* Today, for what things am I most grateful?

Intention - *Lord, open my eyes and ears to be more honest with myself.* Today, what do I really want for myself?

Examination - *Lord, show me what has been happening to me and in me this day.* Today, in what ways have I experienced your love?

Contrition - *Lord, I am still learning to grow in your love.* Today, what choices have been inadequate responses to your love?

Hope - *Lord, let me look with longing toward the future.* Today, how will I let you lead me to a brighter tomorrow?

Musical Selection: *Atmosphere by Luminate*

Day 26 // Stopped to Answer Questions

Scripture Passage: Luke 11:14-28; 11:37-12:12

Jesus spent many hours answering questions about God, the law, and Himself. Jesus never shied away from curious people or hard questions. He always saw it as a way to shape new disciples and point out theological errors within the religious leaders.

Our present world is very gray when it comes to absolute truth. This world tries to convince us that truth for one person is not applicable to another person. The way Jesus handled this was not to ignore the issues, but to answer questions and engage the truth. Jesus never feared people's questions. He welcomed them.

When we are armed with faith in God, we must never fear another's curiosity or their questions about faith. These questions should be welcomed because God places them in their lives to stir their hearts. Most people far from God have questions about God. God uses this curiosity and lack of knowledge for His purposes.

May we listen to people and share in a healthy dialogue with those who believe differently from us. God might be using their curiosity and questions for His purposes.

Musical Selection: *Be Thou My Vision*

Day 27 // Stopped to Call for Repentance

Scripture Passage: Luke 13:1-9

Jesus STOPPED to teach others about the need to repent from sin. Repentance is a spiritual discipline that God wants all of His children to practice. Raise your hand if you have a bad habit! (Come on, no one is around!) Not only do followers of Jesus have bad habits, they have things they do that they do not want to do. This is more than a bad habit, these are sins and they come from our sinful nature. The Greek word for sinful nature is *"jronhma sarkos."* The Apostle Paul says in Romans 7:18, *"For I know that good itself does not dwell in me, that is, in my sinful nature."* Paul states that believers still have a "jronhma sarkos" or "sinful nature." We still have two natures inside of us: a sinful nature and a spiritual nature given by faith in Jesus.

Although sin remains, Jesus reigns in the life of the believer. The truth is that as Christians, we will struggle with sin. We are moving toward perfection but will never realize it until Jesus comes again. God does not leave us to fend for ourselves against the enemy that is sin. The Holy Spirit gives each Christian the power to overcome sin in his or her life. We have the power to fight against temptation and win.

Sin might still happen in our lives, but with repentance, it will never win the war for our souls. When we humbly bring our sin to God in repentance, He reminds us of our value and our worth based on Jesus. He reminds us we never earned our salvation, Jesus earned our salvation; we merely received it as a gift.

May you claim the power that comes with your salvation. May you claim the victory that Jesus has given to you over your sin. May you repent of your sins every day and receive the power of forgiveness.

If Jesus cannot go where sin reigns, and dwell where sin dwells, which is in the heart of every believer, then we have no hope. We have lost our power and our joy of salvation. As the Apostle Paul says, *"Christ in you, the hope of glory,"* and *"Thank God! The answer is in Jesus Christ our Lord."* Jesus has paid the price. He has defeated death and sin. So, repent and believe the good news of Jesus Christ.

Musical Selection: *Lord I Need You*
by Matt Maher

Day 28 // Stopped to Claim Divinity

Scripture Passage: John 10:22-39

Jesus STOPS to claim that He is not just a man, but that He is God. This is one thing that separates Christianity from many other religions, some of which simply believe that Jesus was a great prophet. The belief that Jesus is the messiah is indeed one of the oldest and most central of all Christian beliefs. In Matthew's account of Peter's confession of Jesus, after Jesus asked whom his disciples thought he was, Peter answered, *"You are the Messiah, the Son of the living God."* (Matthew 16:16) The Gospel of Mark is introduced as *"The beginning of the good news of Jesus Christ* (Greek = Christos, either Christ or Messiah), *the Son of God."* (Mark 1:1) Similarly, the author of the Gospel of John says: *"But these are written that you may believe that Jesus is the Messiah, the Son of God, and that by believing you may have life in his name."* (John 20:31)

May you share the good news that the God of Heaven is found in the person of Jesus Christ.

Musical Selection: *Great I Am*
by New Life Worship

Sabbath Day // Stop. Rest. Worship.

"I can safely say, on the authority of all that is revealed in the Word of God, that any man or woman on this earth who is bored and turned off by worship is not ready for heaven."
    - A.W. Tozer

Day 29 // Stopped To Teach #2

Scripture Passage: Luke 13:22-30; 14:7-14

Jesus' ethic was not anything like that of the religious leaders of His time. The Jewish leaders believed that the rich and the powerful were, and should be, favored by God. As Jesus taught His way, He brought a whole new perspective to who is in and who is out. In our scripture for today, He is turning the current state of affairs upside down. Jesus teaches what God's kingdom really looks like, and it includes those who are desolate and lost.

At the beginning of the Sermon on the Mount (Matthew 5-7), in the beatitudes, Jesus has the disciples imagine a different world, a different identity for themselves, a different set of practices, and a different relationship to the status quo. Why would He teach this to His followers? Because it is a picture of God's glorious kingdom.

Who is missing from your Church? Who is not welcome at your place of worship? These are questions we must be asking ourselves as followers of Jesus.

Musical Selection: *Who Am I*
by Casting Crowns

Day 30 // Stopped to Wave at the Fans

Scripture Passage: Luke 14:25-35

Jesus STOPS to test the disciples and the crowds. Jesus wants to know who is a "fan" and who is a "follower." A fan is someone who loves to cheer when everything is going well for the team. A follower is someone who walks with the team when everything has fallen apart and it is not easy.

Every person loves to live in comfort. We live in a consumer culture that sells comfort at every turn. This culture influences our faith more than we think. The Church works hard to create comfortable classes, worship, and service projects, so that people do not need to sacrifice too much time or effort. When a new generation of Christians wants to worship a different way or focus on a different cause, it breaks our comfort. When our comfort is broken, we tend to fight instead of embrace it.

In our scripture passage, Jesus is challenging the comfort levels of the crowd. Were they "fans" of Jesus or "followers" of Jesus? What have we sacrificed for Jesus lately? Are we too comfortable in our faith?

Musical Selection: *Your Name*
by The Digital Age

Day 31 // Stopped to Honor

Scripture Passage: Matthew 19:16-30, Mark 10:17-31, Luke 18:18-30

Jesus STOPS to test once again who is a "fan" and who is a "follower." The Kingdom and the Way that Jesus is teaching about is not like any earthly kingdom or earthly way. This is pyramid living, where Jesus turns everything upside down.

Who are the greatest in the Kingdom of God? The lost, the sick, the last, the servant, the slave, the poor, the desolate, the dependent, the child, the lame, the blind, the diseased, the one who has left everything to follow, the one who is persecuted, and many more found in the Gospels. Every people group on this list is frail and dependent. In God's Kingdom, He receives glory from those who understand that they are frail and weak.

May you see your frailty and dependence as a strength and not as a weakness. May you remember that as a believer you are included in this list. You are the blind person on the side of the road, and you need Jesus every day.

Musical Selection: *In My Weakness*
by Cedars Worship Band

Day 32 // Stopped to be Anointed

Scripture Passage: Matthew 26:6-13,
Mark 14:3-9, John 12:1-11

Jesus STOPPED on His way to the cross to be anointed. This anointing was a self-less act by a woman who had nothing else to offer Jesus. The perfume she used was probably worth a year's wages, and it could have feed many hungry and homeless people. Judas saw the frivolousness of the offering and called Jesus on it.

Let us look closer at the action and not so much the act. The act of pouring out an expensive perfume was reckless. But the action of pouring out the expensive perfume was price-less. This woman was pouring herself out to Jesus. She was not going to hide who she was anymore from anyone. In his play *Macbeth*, William Shakespeare writes, *"God hath given you one face, and you make yourselves another."*

Jesus wants to free us from our false self and the masks we hide behind. May you let Him!

Musical Selection: *Alabaster Jar*
by Gateway Worship

Day 33 // Stopped to Ride a Donkey

Scripture Passage: Matthew 21:1-11,
Mark 11:1-11, Luke 19:28-44, John 12:12-19

Have you ever been embarrassed? Really embarrassed? Like forgot-to-wear-your-clothes-to-school dream embarrassed? If you are living life, you will feel embarrassed at some point. Do you think Jesus' disciples felt embarrassed when He chose a donkey to ride triumphantly into Jerusalem on? Actually, they did not feel this way. Jesus was fulfilling a 500-year-old prophecy by choosing a donkey. For centuries it had been believed that this was the way the Messiah would ride into the City of David.

When Jesus STOPS to ride on a donkey, He is proclaiming His divinity and His messiah-ship to the nations gathered in Jerusalem. Christian tradition marks Jesus' ride as the start of Holy Week. Holy Week is a journey that takes each believer through a range of emotions. It is a road that we must travel every year at this time.

May you experience the excitement of the Messiah riding into Jerusalem, and may you feel the joy of the people shouting, "Hosanna."

In order to experience the joy of Easter, we need to experience the gut-wrenching heartache of Jesus on the cross. Take time to free your busy schedule this coming week, and experience all Holy Week has to offer at your church. The experiences will truly make Easter feel like a day of Resurrection!

Musical Selection: *Hosanna*
by Lincoln Brewster

Day 34 // Stopped to be the Good News

Scripture Passage: John 12:20-50

Jesus STOPS and again spends time with the Jewish leaders, the disciples, and the crowds. Jesus is not only sharing the Good News, He *is* the Good News. Still, some people simply cannot recognize Him. Within the week, Jesus is going to be crucified on a cross for all those gathered around Him. His greatest desire is for their hearts to recognize Him for who He is. In verses 35 and 36, Jesus tells them, "You are going to have the light just a little while longer. Walk while you have the light, before darkness overtakes you. Whoever walks in the dark does not know where they are going. Believe in the light while you have the light, so that you may become children of light."

May you remember to share the Good News of Jesus by walking in the Light. May you know Jesus is being radiated from your life because you believe in Him. Claim it and live it!

Musical Selection: *Shadows*
by Passion Worship Band

Sabbath Day // Stop. Rest. Worship.

"God is spirit, and his worshipers must worship in the Spirit and in truth."

- Jesus of Nazareth

Day 35 // Stopped to Prepare

Scripture Passage: Matthew 21:12-17, Mark 11:15-19, Luke 19:45-48

Jesus STOPS to prepare the temple to receive the Good News. The Jewish temple was the heart of the sacrificial system. The temple was not a place of worship, but had become a business for the religious leaders. The temple did not house the Ark of the Covenant anymore. The Ark had been lost in the Babylonian invasion and was never seen again. The temple contained the Holy Place and the Holy of Holies. The Ark of the Covenant (the symbolic presence of God) was usually housed in the Holy of Holies. The current temple did not have the presence of God in the Holy of Holies.

The presence of God was in the very midst of the people in a person: Jesus. The temple and its leaders have become so corrupt that they do not even recognize the presence of God when it is before them. Jesus clears out the moneychangers in an effort to refocus the people on God's presence.

On the day Jesus dies, the temple veil (curtain) that separates the people from the Holy of Holies is torn in two. Jesus is the ultimate sacrifice for all time, and He is the ultimate act of intercession between God and humankind. Jesus removes the veil (curtain) and gives each person who believes full access to the presence of God.

Do you feel God's presence in your life? You should! Remember that as a believer you are a carrier of God's presence. You are the new Holy of Holies and that is the greatest privilege a person could ever have.

Musical Selection: *Enter this Temple*
by Leeland

Day 36 // Stopped to Curse

Scripture Passage: Matthew 21:18-22,
Mark 11:12-14, 20-25

Jesus STOPS and performs His last miracle in the gospels. His last miracle is cursing a fig tree and making it die. That does not seem like a very good representation of His ministry or His time, does it? There is, of course, a deeper meaning to Jesus' work.

The barren fig tree symbolizes the spiritually dead Jewish leaders. They did not like the Son of God in their presence or in their temple. Jesus' action announces the end of the spiritual leadership of this current temple. Forty years after Jesus' death, the temple and the leadership were ultimately destroyed.

The new spiritual leaders of God's kingdom will learn to trust God and enter into an intimate relationship with Him. By doing so, they will have God's will revealed to them.

Musical Selection: *This I Know*
by New Life Worship

Day 37 // Stopped to be a Servant

Scripture Passage: John 13:1-20

Did you notice that without the gospel of John, we would never have known Jesus washed His disciple's feet?

Jesus STOPS on His way to the cross to be a servant. Jesus has always modeled servant-leadership and one of His last actions to His disciples is to serve them. If we look at when this took place, it makes the action even more profound.

Have you ever had an important event you were getting ready for? Have you ever had an event like a surgery or a hard conversation at work that was going to take place the next day? When these things are present in our lives, we are not very servant-oriented and we tend to think about our own wants and needs. Jesus did the exact opposite. He thought about others, even at the apex of His betrayal and future crucifixion.

Remember, as disciples of Jesus, we are called to be servant-leaders. May our lives be a reflection of our Savior and Lord.

Musical Selection: *Here I am Lord*

Day 38 // Stopped to be Crucified

Scripture Passage: Matthew 27:35-56,
Mark 15:24-41, Luke 23:33-49, John 19:18-37

Jesus STOPS to share in the Passover meal with His disciples. One of them betrays Him, and He is arrested, flogged, and sentenced to death. This is the story of the Savior of the World.

Jesus goes to the cross so that all humankind may be redeemed and delivered from their sins. The God of the universe puts Himself on a cross because He loves His creation. Remember what John 3:16 says: *"For God so loved the world that he gave his one and only Son, that whoever believes in him shall not perish but have eternal life."*

There have been books, songs, painting, and plays written and created about Jesus' act of love on the cross. There is not enough paper in the entire world to explain how significant this act is for all humanity and those who believe Jesus to be their Savior.

May this week be a reminder of all God has done for you. May the images of the cross move you to worship Jesus Christ.

Musical Selection: *Above All
by Michael W. Smith*

Day 39 // Stopped to be Laid in a Tomb

Scripture Passage: Matthew 27:57-61,
Mark 15:42-47, Luke 23:50-56, John 19:38-42

    Jesus might have STOPPED there, but He only stayed for three days. He is not there anymore!

Musical Selection: *Overcome*
by New Life Worship

Day 40 // Stopped to be Resurrected

Scripture Passage: Matthew 27:35-56,
Mark 15:24-41, Luke 23:33-49, John 19:18-37

Jesus STOPPED on this pale blue dot in the middle of the Milky Way galaxy to live, to minister, to die, and to be resurrected, so that all creation could be redeemed. The God of the universe STOPPED off to heal a beggar, to love a sinner, to call a group of followers, and to bring life to spiritually dead things.

No matter how hard we try in our lives, we cannot bring life to that which is dead. Easter and the resurrection of Jesus is the confirmation that we cannot save ourselves. The moment an individual recognizes that only One, Jesus, can bring life to that which is dead, eternal life will be theirs forever. The moment that we realize that Jesus defeated death, that He paid the price, that He did the work, and that by His resurrection we can know the love and grace of God, in that moment we are forever saved. We are made new in Him.

May we recognize this not just once a year, but also encounter this truth daily. May we devote our lives to serving Jesus and loving like He loved. May we realize that the power that raised Jesus from the dead now lives in all believers.

May the words of the Apostle Paul from Ephesians 1:7-14 ring true in our hearts and in our lives...

7 So overflowing is his kindness toward us that he took away all our sins through the blood of his Son, by whom we are saved; 8 and he has showered down upon us the richness of his grace—for how well he understands us and knows what is best for us at all times.

9 God has told us his secret reason for sending Christ, a plan he decided on in mercy long ago; 10 and this was his purpose: that when the time is ripe he will gather us all together from wherever we are—in heaven or on earth—to be with him in Christ forever. 11 Moreover, because of what Christ has done, we have become gifts to God that he delights in, for as part of God's sovereign plan we were chosen from the beginning to be his, and all things happen just as he decided long ago. 12 God's purpose in this was that we should praise God and give glory to him for doing these mighty things for us, who were the first to trust in Christ.

13 And because of what Christ did, all you others too, who heard the Good News about how to be saved, and trusted Christ, were marked as belonging to Christ by the Holy Spirit, who long ago had been promised to all of us Christians. 14 His presence within us is God's guarantee that he really will give us all that he promised; and the Spirit's seal upon us means that God has already purchased us and that he guarantees to bring us to himself. This is just one more reason for us to praise our glorious God.

Musical Selection: *Hallelujah Chorus*

Closing Acknowledgements

Thank you to Dustin Delong for the help in selecting our musical offerings for the devotional book.

Thank you to Jim and Janet Chase for the use of their lake house for the writing and compiling of this devotional book.

Thanks again to Jesus, who STOPPED in my heart and got stuck.

www.ingramcontent.com/pod-product-compliance
Lightning Source LLC
Chambersburg PA
CBHW060418050426
42449CB00009B/2013

* 9 7 8 0 6 1 5 9 6 2 4 5 0 *